Towle Mfg. Company

The colonial Book of the Towle Mfg. Co.

Towle Mfg. Company

The colonial Book of the Towle Mfg. Co.

ISBN/EAN: 9783337153953

Printed in Europe, USA, Canada, Australia, Japan

Cover: Foto ©ninafisch / pixelio.de

More available books at **www.hansebooks.com**

NEWBURYPORT, 1697. Whittier.
UP AND DOWN THE VILLAGE STREETS
STRANGE ARE THE FORMS MY FANCY
    MEETS,
FOR THE THOUGHTS AND THINGS OF
    TO-DAY ARE HID,
AND THROUGH THE VEIL OF A CLOSED
    LID
THE ANCIENT WORTHIES I SEE AGAIN.

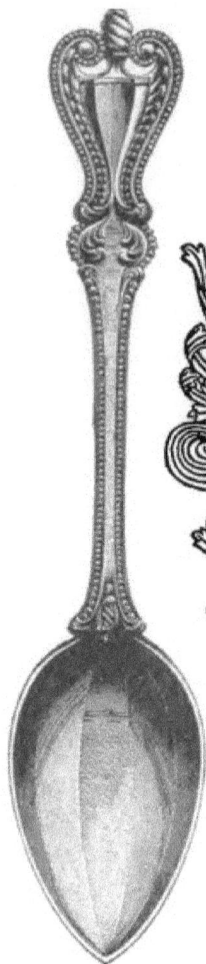

The
𝔠𝔬𝔩𝔬𝔫𝔦𝔞𝔩
𝔅𝔬𝔬𝔨
of the
TOWLE MFG. CO.

Which is intended to De-
lineate and Describe some
Quaint and *Historic* Places
in NEWBURYPORT and Vicinity
and show the *Origin* and
Beauty of the COLONIAL
Pattern of Silverware.

NEWBURYPORT

THE history of Newburyport is variously written, and, in a way, completely recorded; but this mass of material, precious as it is, only suggests the wealth of romance centering about the old town, locked up in journals and log-books, or fading away in the memories of the few relics of earlier and more picturesque times.

The ideals of to-day, here as everywhere else, are properly business and progress on the lines of modern opportunities; and this is the same spirit of enterprise which led our progenitors of seventy-five or one hundred years ago to their undertakings by sea and land, and brought them riches and renown in such generous measure.

That they are interesting and picturesque is merely incidental; their purpose was as matter-of-fact and practical as any to-day, and as well attained ; but time and changed customs lend charm to their personalities, while many of their deeds are records of bravery and greatness that would be memorable under any conditions.

Going back still further, to its first settlement in 1635, on the banks of the Parker river, called by the Indians Quascacunquen and renamed by the settlers in honor of their spiritual leader, we see a band of sturdy voyagers giving up the comforts of life in the mother country for the rugged hardships of a wilderness, and between them a long and tedious passage over a stormy sea in the small vessels and with the scant knowledge of that day. Some of them had the previous summer journeyed from Boston to Ipswich, then the outpost, where they were joined by later arrivals; and traveling by land even for so short a distance being

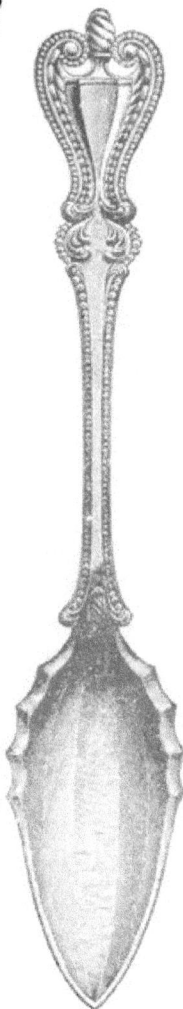

difficult, they loaded their goods in open boats and followed t[o] shore to the pleasant haven which had been selected for th[eir] home. They were not needy nor driven to this step for a live[li]hood, as one of their first acts was stock raising on an extensi[ve] scale with cattle imported from Holland, and in the compa[ny] were graduates of Oxford University. They soon establishe[d] a thriving "plantation," as it was then termed, and were ear[ly] incorporated and represented by deputy at the General Cou[rt] held in Boston to administer the affairs of Massachusetts Bay.

If we would realize the strength of purpose which sustaine[d] these colonists, we must picture the conditions which confronte[d] them. The severity of New England winter; their isolati[on] and lack of material resources, for almost everything must [be] laboriously wrought out; their danger from wild beasts an[d] hostile Indians; and the uncertainty of those crops which mea[nt] so much for their good or ill.

That they persevered and succeeded, Newburyport is the ev[i]dence; but the story of their trials and achievements is a reproac[h] to the easy critic of the present, who reaps with little labo[r] benefits for which they struggled and hoped, but of which, f[or] the most part, they had little comprehension.

That they were devout people needs no saying, their publi[c] religious worship commencing under a spreading tree, the firs[t] Sunday after their arrival. That they also recognized the need of the body as well as the soul, is evidenced by the licens[e] granted by the General Court to one of the settlers, within si[x] months of their arrival, to keep an ordinary, or inn, for th[e] entertainment of such as needed. This community was early i[n] establishing important enterprises which, with the systemati[c] parceling out of the land and the development and managemen[t] of current affairs, gave them abundant occupation and shows their remarkable energy and business capacity. The descendant[s] of these pioneers occupy practically the same lands to-day, which are among the most prosperous farms of the region.

The growth of the town was to the northward, and soon from the shelter of the "Oldtown" hills the settlement stretched

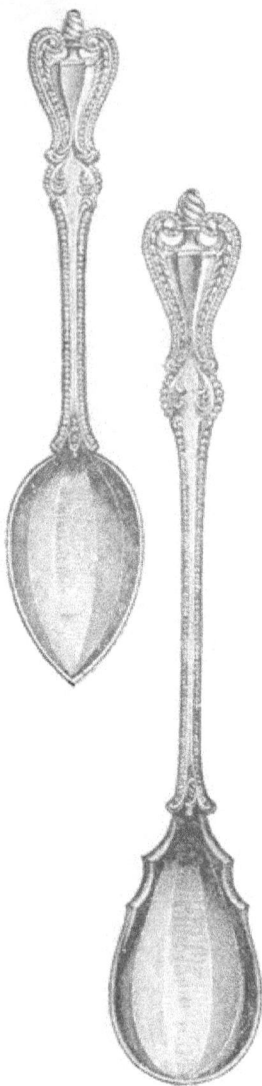

The Colonial Book

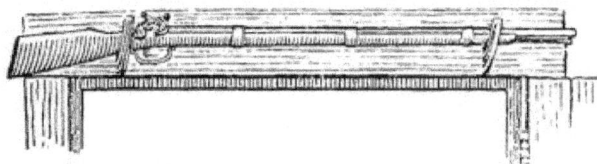

along the bank of the Merrimac, and, embracing eagerly the opportunities it offered, encouraged maritime enterprises in every way, until with the building of wharves and the establishment of ship-yards began the era which was to give to Newburyport its real power and position. The small vessels for fishing became numerous, and were followed by larger and more pretentious craft, which carried to foreign ports the products of the country, and brought back the rich goods and outfittings needed in the rapidly developing community, or distributed through surrounding and inland towns.

Through this commerce came wealth and culture, and many are the evidences of magnificent living among the rich merchants, while the numerous ship-masters returned from foreign lands with minds broadened and stimulated by contact with other peoples and tastes formed which greatly modified the old Puritan customs.

The town furnished many troops for the Colonial and Indian wars, and was foremost in the demonstration against the Stamp Act, also heartily supporting the Revolutionary war from the first Lexington alarm. In these troops were officers of high rank whose deeds of valor are national history.

The naval forces were greatly strengthened by ships built here, and from here also numerous privateers sailed with letters of marque and returned with rich prizes to be in turn fitted out

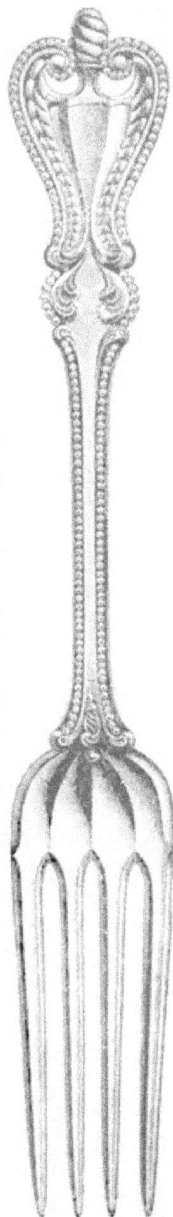

View of River Front and Shipping

on the same errands. Many are the thrilling tales of capture, imprisonment, and escape told by the returning heroes, and it is small wonder that with the prospect of booty and adventure active young men took naturally to the sea.

Commercial activity suffered a severe blow in the embargo placed on foreign trade by the government in 1807, and while it lasted shipping was at a complete standstill. A few years later, in 1811, came a second misfortune, in the form of the great fire which in one night destroyed sixteen acres of the business district, including nearly all the important public buildings and institutions. Though in a measure soon recovered from, these calamities served to seriously check advancing prosperity, and while later there were large importing interests they failed to reach their former importance, and have now, with changed methods of transportation, almost entirely disappeared. In their place have come mills and factories with their attendant needs and influences, bringing a larger if not a wealthier population, and it is by these that the city must continue to thrive.

The manufacture of silverware is one of these factors, which, having its beginning as shown by authentic record in the modest

Dalton House

The Colonial Book

enterprise of William Moulton in 1689, has steadily developed until it is now one of the most important industries; and it is especially fitting that a Colonial pattern of spoons and like table-ware should be produced where one of the first silversmiths of the country worked, and established a business which has been continued without interruption to the present day.

It is interesting to note in this connection that here was born Jeremiah Dummer, who, in 1659, was apprenticed to John Hull of Boston, one of the early settlers of that place and the first silversmith in America. Jeremiah Dummer, who was thus the first native American to practise this art, was afterward judge of the Court of Common Pleas of Suffolk County, and was the father of William Dummer, governor of the Province of Massachusetts.

Another Newburyport silversmith who attained prominence outside his profession was Jacob Perkins, who, in 1781, at the age of fifteen, was by the death of his master left in charge of his business, and who at twenty-one was employed to make dies for the Massachusetts Mint. He afterward became famous as an inventor, and removed to London, where his genius was recognized by the Society of Liberal Arts, and he was rewarded with their medals.

During this eventful history many men have arisen here to be enrolled among the world's acknowledged benefactors, and a few of these were noticed on another page, in connection with the places enriched by their remembrance.

The growing interest in such matters fostered by historical societies, improvement societies, and the various organizations of descendants of Revolutionary patriots, is a marked sign of the times, and to such it is hoped these pages will appeal; while to those who may visit Newburyport, they will serve as an introduction: and others, far away, may realize some of the beauties and attractions of this old New England city.

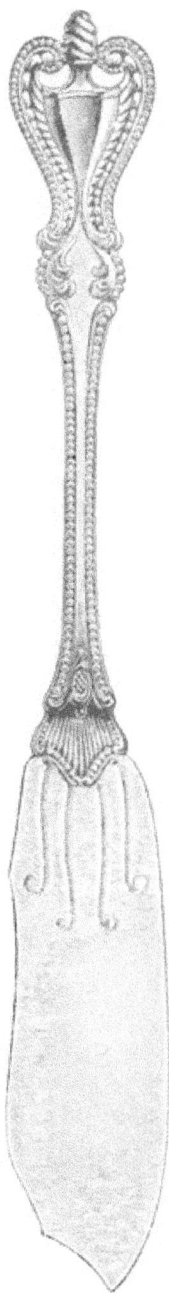

The Colonial Book

THE EARLY WARS.

IN the foregoing sketch we have briefly touched upon the part of Old Newbury, and later, Newburyport, in our country's early wars. Their record in the establishment and defence of our National government can be but outlined here, yet however incomplete this account, it seems fit at a time of such wide awaking to the glory of our past, when individuals recall with justifiable pride the services of patriotic ancestors, that the brilliant accomplishments, and also the not less glorious though unavailing efforts of a community, be indicated for the many to whom the full history is not available.

In the early expeditions against hostile Indians, Newbury took an important part, from the Pequod war two years after her settlement, in which she furnished one-fifteenth of the Massachusetts quota; the King Philip war, in which more than one-half her eligible inhabitants were enlisted; the French and Indian war, when a part of her expedition against Cape Breton was cast away and lost; to the war with the Norridgewocks, which was terminated by the killing of Sebastian Ralle, their French leader, by Lieut. Jaques of this town.

During the frequent wars between France and England, while this country was still a colony, many men went from here, to fight in England's cause on the Canadian frontier. Chief among those were Col. Moses Titcomb, Capt. William Davenport, and Nathaniel Knapp. The former, serving in many campaigns under Sir William Pepperell, took part in the capture of Louisburg and the battle of Crown Point, where he was shot while directing his regiment in most effective operations. Capt. Davenport raised companies and served in two campaigns, being with Gen. Wolfe on the plains of Abraham, and a few days later at the surrender of Quebec.

It was reserved, however, for the thrilling issues of the war of independence to call forth the universal and unwavering patriotism of the residents of old Newbury.

The story of pre-revolutionary agitation in Newburyport is one of steadily threatening protest, from the first application of

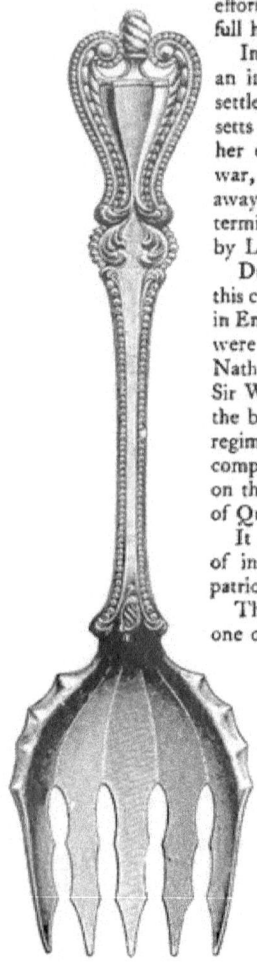

the Stamp Act. As early as 1765 a stamp distributor was hung in effigy, while visiting strangers were subjected to rough handling, if they were not quick to proclaim their antipathy to this measure. Such treatment was perforce exercised upon strangers, if at all, as in this town only four persons were suspected of loyalism and of these there was proof against but one, who died before the call to war which would have revealed his position. This was a record perhaps unequalled.

From that time to the actual outbreak of hostilities, Newburyport was in a ferment of restrained rebellion; this unity of opinion and harmony of action would have been impossible in a lesser cause, and was the more remarkable when we consider that such action meant the sacrifice of a large part of the town's greatest interest, her commerce and its dependent shipbuilding, and that the rejection of British goods meant the retirement of the many vessels in that trade.

This was the actual result ; but instead of turning the people from their elected course it added to their determination, and they organized to prevent possible smuggling of the detested commodities. Under the wise and temperate leadership of the Committee of Safety, they corresponded with neighboring towns and the remoter colonies, and when the first blow was struck at Lexington it found them ready and impatient for the great struggle for civil liberty.

It was eleven o'clock at night on the nineteenth of April, 1775, when the courier bearing news of the fight at Lexington reached this town; but not a moment was lost, and before midnight the first detachment of minute-men was galloping over the road, while morning found four companies on the way to the scene of conflict. At the termination of this alarm these companies returned, but others were soon formed for regular service in the Continental army, and did memorable work at the battle of Bunker Hill.

At Whittier's Birth Place.

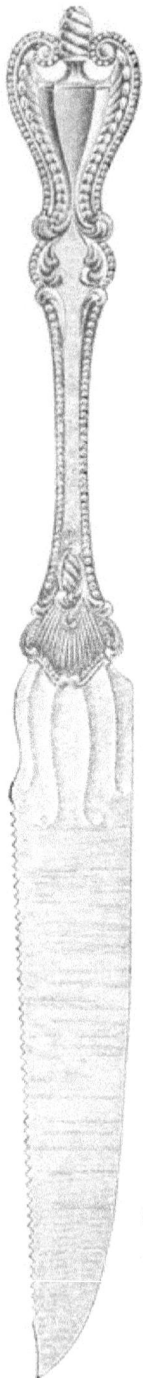

The Colonial Book

Space forbids following these troops through this and other battles, but a few figures rise pre-eminent, and no account, however slight, would be complete without them.

Col. Moses Little was in command of a regiment in many important battles of the Revolution, beginning with Bunker Hill, where he was officer of the day when Washington took command. On account of ill health brought on in the service, he declined the commission of brigadier general, and the command of a special expedition raised by the Commonwealth of Massachusetts.

Col. Edward Wigglesworth was appointed to a regiment early in 1776, and served with distinction for three years, when he was retired at his own request. He took a prominent part in Arnold's expedition on Lake Champlain, being third in command, and materially aided the retreat of the flotilla when it was hemmed in by the enemy.

Captain, afterward Major, Ezra Lunt was another who served at Bunker Hill, and it is asserted that his company was formed in the broad aisle of the Old South church at the close of a sermon, in response to the pastor's appeal for volunteers; and that it was the first volunteer company of the Continental army.

Here formed and embarked the important expedition under Benedict Arnold, then a valued officer in the patriot army, which, penetrating to Quebec, assisted Montgomery in his gallant assault.

As it was with maritime affairs that Newburyport was chiefly identified, it is to the sea that we must look for her most brilliant and individual victories.

Congress soon realized that our shipping was being rapidly exterminated by the armed vessels of the enemy, and issued letters of marque to assist the feeble and barely established navy in retaliating for these encroachments; ship owners here were not slow to accept these privileges, and many privateers were fitted out and manned, often by the flower of the town's youth; one

Devil's Den

of these, the Yankee Hero, the second of that name, sailing in 1775 under Capt. James Tracy, with twenty guns and a crew of one hundred and seventy men, including fifty from Newburyport's first families, was never afterward heard from.

The spirit that animated these bold mariners may be judged from the announcement made on the occasion of prayers in church for the success of the Game Cock, the first privateer to sail out of any port, that she hoped to "scour the coast of our unnatural enemies," though she was a sloop of but twenty-four tons. She sailed from Newburyport in August, 1775, and succeeded in bringing prizes into port.

It would be difficult to estimate the number of these privateers, but that they were numerous and successful will be understood when it is stated that twenty-four ships of which Mr. Nathaniel Tracy was principal owner, with a tonnage of 6,330 and carrying 2,800 men, captured from the enemy one hundred and twenty vessels amounting to 23,360 tons, and which with their cargoes were sold for three million nine hundred and fifty thousand specie dollars. Mr. Tracy was also principal owner in one hundred and ten other vessels, twenty-three of which were letters of marque. These vessels were closely allied to the regular navy, which was now gaining strength, and we find the same men alternating between the command of privateers and government vessels, as the fortunes of war permitted.

The frigates Boston, Hancock, and Protection, and the brig Pickering, were built here, as well as the sloop of war Merrimac which was built by subscription and tendered to the government, when its funds were reduced, to be paid for at a very low price

Plum Island

Col Barrett House Concord

when convenient. She was commanded by Capt. Moses Brown
of this port, a remarkably gallant sailor, and during the five years
that she was in commission made many important captures.

The war ships Alliance and Warren were also built on the
Merrimac, just above Newburyport, and were fitted out at this
place.

The name of Paul Jones, the intrepid and irresistible "Citizen
of the World," as he later styled himself, whose brilliant prowess
was developed in the service of the United States, is connected
with Newburyport through two of his ablest lieutenants, Henry
and Cutting Lunt.

The messieurs Lunt, cousins, first shipped in the brig Dalton,
Captain Eleazer Johnston, which sailed, with a crew of one
hundred and twenty men, November 15, 1776. The Dalton
was captured, the twenty-fourth of the following December, by
the sixty-four-gun man-of-war Reasonable, of the English navy,
and her crew cast into Mill Prison, Plymouth, where they remained, and suffered great hardships, for more than two years,
and were finally released through the efforts of Benjamin Franklin.
During this time Charles Herbert of Newburyport, one of the
number, wrote a journal which he preserved in spite of the close
inspection to which they were subjected. After his death this
journal was published, and forms a most interesting and valuable
record of life in an English prison.

Henry and Cutting Lunt, on obtaining their liberty, went to
France and enlisted as midshipmen with Paul Jones, on the *Bon
Homme Richard* then fitting out at L'Orient. They were speedily
promoted lieutenants, and served their able commander, whom
they greatly admired, in many of his fiercest engagements, in-

The Colonial Book

cluding that with the Serapis. It was in this terrible battle, when Commodore Jones was fighting against heavy odds, that his success was almost reversed by the traitorous act of his subordinate, the Frenchman Landais. The latter was in command of the ship Alliance before mentioned, and, inspired by jealousy, continued under the presumable excuse of firing at the enemy, to rake the decks of the *Bon Homme Richard*, in spite of the frantic signals of the latter. Many Newburyport men were in the crew of the Alliance at that time, and were thus obliged to fire on their friends and townsmen.

When Paul Jones was recruiting for a frigate building for him at Portsmouth, he came to Newburyport to engage Henry Lunt, and expressed great regret when he found that Lieutenant Lunt had sailed on the letter of marque ship Intrepid, of this port. He remarked that he would prefer Mr. Lunt to any officer he had ever known.

Many seamen from Newburyport also served under Jones in the Ranger, *Bon Homme Richard*, Alliance, and Ariel.

While men-of-war and privateers carried brave men to seek the enemy abroad, those left at home were far from idle. Shipbuilding was very active, forts were established and maintained at the mouth of the river, while the English ship Friends, which had mistaken this port for Boston, was captured off the bar, by the stratagem of adventurous spirits who had observed her actions from the town and boarded her in open boats.

In 1779 the ship Vengeance and the schooner Shark fitted out here and joined the ill-fated expedition by which it was intended to overthrow the British military post on the Penobscot, but which, after entering the harbor, was hemmed in by a large fleet

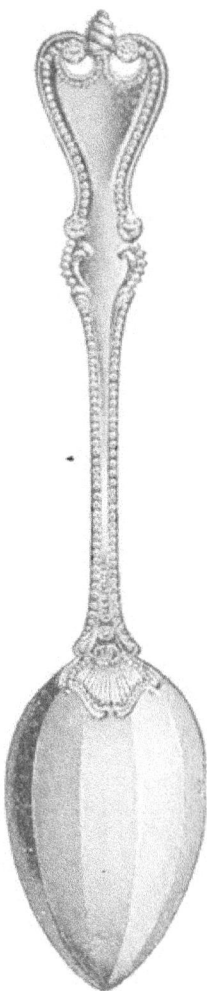

The Colonial Book

of the enemies' ships, that appeared unexpectedly. Rather than see them fall into the hands of the British, the commander of the expedition ordered his ships burned, and the crews found their way home overland.

The war of 1812 found Newburyport just recovering from the great fire of 1811, and the paralyzing Embargo of previous years. In striking contrast to their war spirit in the Revolution, the people of this town were almost unanimously opposed to this second war with England, and this not for reasons of mere commercial policy, however much they needed business, but on the ground that such a war was unjustified, and that the differences might easily be settled in other ways. An address adopted in full town meeting was sent to the legislature of Massachusetts, in which they declared their willingness to stand by the Constitution and defend their rights, and their equal unwillingness to take any aggressive part in the proposed war. These sentiments were in the main adhered to, throughout hostilities, and in pursuance of them, forts were manned at the mouth of the Merrimac and at other points on Plum Island, which served to keep at bay several English ships that hovered around this part of the coast, in the hope of destroying the sloop of war Wasp and gunboats Number Eighty-one and Number Eighty-three, then building here.

Although privateering shared to a great degree the unpopularity of the war, quite a number were fitted out here, some of which made brilliant records. Chief among these was the brig Decatur, Captain William Nichols, which, during two weeks of one voyage, captured eight vessels, four of which were armed. Earlier in the war Captain Nichols was in command of the merchant ship Alert, which was taken by the British man-of-war Semramis, and ordered to Plymouth under a guard from the latter. Before reaching that port, however, Captain Nichols

Old town Hill and Parker River Bridge

and his men regained control of the ship and imprisoned the British seamen in the hold. Unfortunately, they soon fell in with another British ship, the Vestal, which again took them and carried them to Portsmouth, England. This may have determined Captain Nichols to his latter course which was of undoubted service to the National cause.

Privateering, though apparently very remunerative during the war of the Revolution, did not prove so in the end, except as it stimulated business for the time being, and the enormous fortunes gained by individuals were much reduced by later losses and contributions to the expense of war. In addition to the many merchant ships captured by the English, twenty-two vessels, carrying over one thousand men, sailed from here and were never afterward heard from.

In the eight years from the battle of Lexington to the proclamation of peace, Newburyport raised for current expenses $2,522,500, which was eighty-five times the aggregate of appropriations for an equal period immediately preceding.

It was at first intended to print here the names of all who served in the Revolutionary wars, from Newbury and Newburyport, but the impossibility of this becomes apparent when we find that in the neighborhood of fifteen hundred were in the army alone, at one time or another; while the number of those that were in the navy or privateers would be difficult even to estimate. In place of this, the publishers of this book will freely send to any of Newbury or Newburyport ancestry, all available record of any name submitted, or will, in any other way possible, identify early patriots.

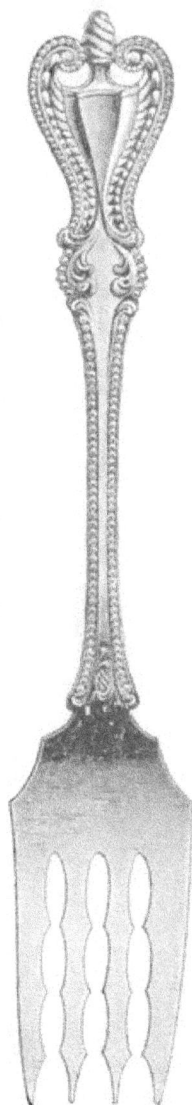

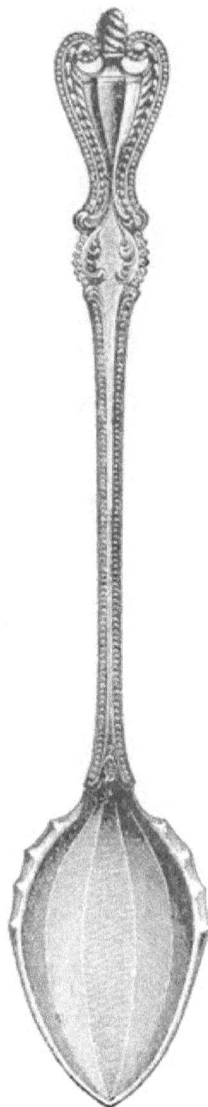

The Colonial Book

ALTHOUGH commerce and ship-building were the chief industrial interests of Newburyport in its early years, invention and manufacturing were by no means absent. Reference has been made to the antiquity of silversmithing here, and much more might be said of the extent of this industry, and the variety of articles manufactured. Some of them, as for instance silver shoe-buckles, are now obsolete, while silver thimbles and necklaces of gold beads, though still used, are not commonly the product of silversmiths. In 1824, machinery was invented here for the manufacture of silver thimbles, and an extensive business was developed in this line, but it has long since ceased to exist.

Many instances might be cited of great men who were trained as gold or silversmiths, but whose talents afterwards enriched other branches of art or science. In the old world, Cellini and Michael Angelo were prominent examples, and, later, Paul Revere arose in this country and rendered important services for the welfare, comfort, and prosperity of a struggling people. In like manner, Jacob Perkins, the Newburyport silversmith, whose great skill as engraver and die-cutter, as well as silversmith, is elsewhere referred to, was too richly endowed with ideas and ambition to limit his efforts to a narrow field.

He was born July 9, 1766, and died July 13, 1849, after a life of versatile activity in the mechanic arts and sciences, where, in the face of triumphs that would have satisfied many, we find him turning from one problem to another, and gaining new laurels from each. One of his most important inventions was a machine for making nails, produced when he was but twenty-four years of age. At that time all nails were forged by hand, and a good workman could produce one thousand in a day. With his perfected machines, the daily product of one man was increased to ten kegs, of one hundred pounds each.

He associated with himself Messrs Guppy & Armstrong of Newburyport, who built the machines, and together they estab-

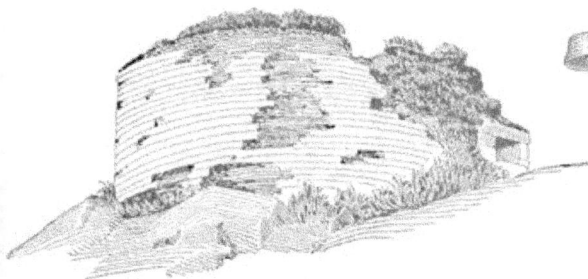

Wallach Tower Newcastle

lished a manufactory at Newbury Falls, a part of the town now called Byfield, where water-power was available.

In the following extract from an advertisement in the Impartial Herald, Newburyport, 1795, we catch a glimpse of business methods in those days of quaint customs:—

The patentee would inform the public that they have begun the manufacture of brads, and will have a considerable number in fourteen or twenty days. As some will naturally think they cannot supply the whole continent and will therefore order from abroad, they would say that they have three engines which will make thirty-six hundred thousand weekly, and will add one engine each month.

N. B. A few whitesmiths may have constant employ and liberal wages.

Proprietors { Jacob Perkins, Inventor. { Guppy & Armstrong.

To follow in detail all the enterprises and achievements of Jacob Perkins would unduly extend this article, and we can only briefly refer to the most important.

He invented a stereotype check-plate for the reverse of bank-bills, designed for the prevention of counterfeiting. This was very successful, there being no record of an attempt to counterfeit it, whereas the practice had been very common with those previously used.

During the war of 1812, he was employed by the National government in the construction of machinery for boring out old and honey-combed cannon, and he invented a steam gun that discharged one thousand balls a minute.

He made great improvements in hardening and softening steel and particularly applied these to the engraving of that metal.

He demonstrated the compressibility of water, inventing the Piezometer for this purpose, and invented instruments for measuring the depth of the sea. On his arrival in London in 1820, he published a treatise on these subjects. He also experimented on new types of the steam engine, in some employ-

Peter Parton

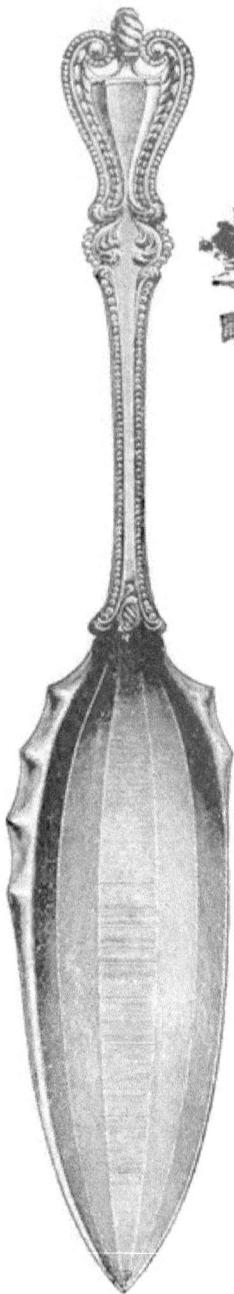

ing steam at a pressure of 65 atmospheres, or 975 pounds to the square inch.

To him all phenomena and conditions seem to have been a challenge, and he applied his powers to the solution of any problem presented. In London he was known as the "American Inventor," and was accorded much distinction.

Another industry inaugurated by Newburyport capital was located at the falls in Byfield. This was the Newburyport Woolen Company, established in 1794, the first company incorporated for that business in the state, and by some authorities named as the first woolen manufactory in America. The carding and other machines for its equipment were built by Standring, Guppy, & Armstrong, in Newburyport, being set up in "Lord" Timothy Dexter's stable; and were the first made in this country.

At Newbury a fulling mill had been in operation since 1687, when it was established by Peter Cheney, who sold it to John Pearson, by whose descendants it was operated as a fulling mill and blanket factory until destroyed by fire. It was succeeded by the present mill, established by the Pearsons, who are most prominently identified with this industry.

At Byfield, also, machinery for making wooden shoe-pegs was invented by Paul Pillsbury. This article completely revolutionized the manufacture.

Other industries that at the beginning of this century contributed largely to Newburyport's prosperity, were:—cordage-making, employing fifty hands; boot and shoe making (Newbury and Newburyport together), employing upwards of one hundred and fifty hands, these being scattered in the little shops that dotted the country in that day; comb-making, the product of which was nearly $200,000, annually; tobacco-manufacture, in the form of snuffs and cigars; tanning; morocco-dressing; wool-pulling; carriage-building; and not least of all, distilling. Rum was a very important commodity, freely drunk by high and low; and few advertisements of merchandise were seen without the announcement of a choice hogshead of rum, generally in large type at the head of the list.

At the close of the last century there were ten distilleries in active operation here, contributing to the reputation of New England rum.

Another notable feature was Newburyport's importance as a publishing centre, and the extent of its retail book-trade.

The first newspaper here was established in 1773, by Isaiah Thomas and Henry W. Tinges, who, on December 4 of that year, issued the first number of the Essex Journal and New Hampshire Packet.

Only a few of the books published here can be alluded to, but some of these were of much importance.

The first system of Arithmetic published in this country was the work of Nicholas Pike, a Newburyport school-master, and was published here in 1787. This was a very comprehensive work, and was an authority for many years.

Blunt's famous "Coast Pilot" and other nautical works were published here by Blunt & March, who also issued many other volumes, including medical works, Bibles, Testaments, hymn books, and other religious works, such as "Christ's Famous Titles and Believer's Golden Chain, together with Cabinet of Jewels."

Other works were: Quarles' "Emblems and Hieroglyphics of the Life of Man," 1799, with copperplate engravings; "The Life of Nelson;" "The Life of Paul Jones;" "The Poetical Works of Peter Pindar, a Distant Relation of the Poet of

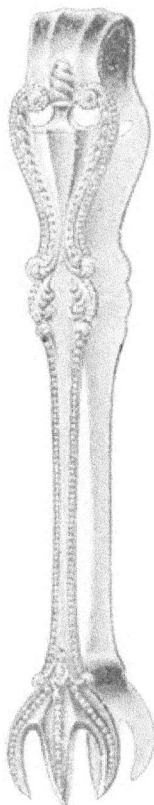

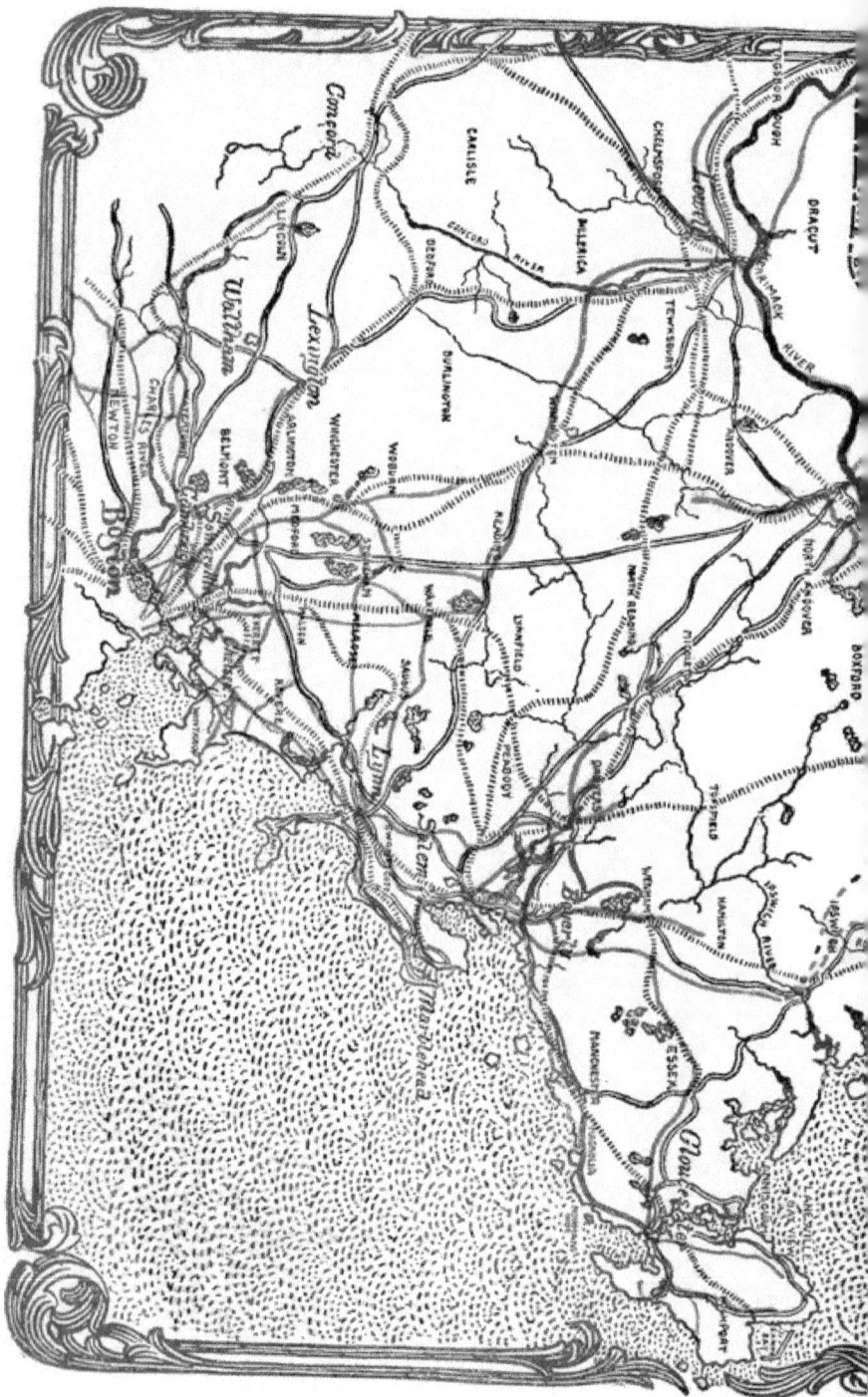

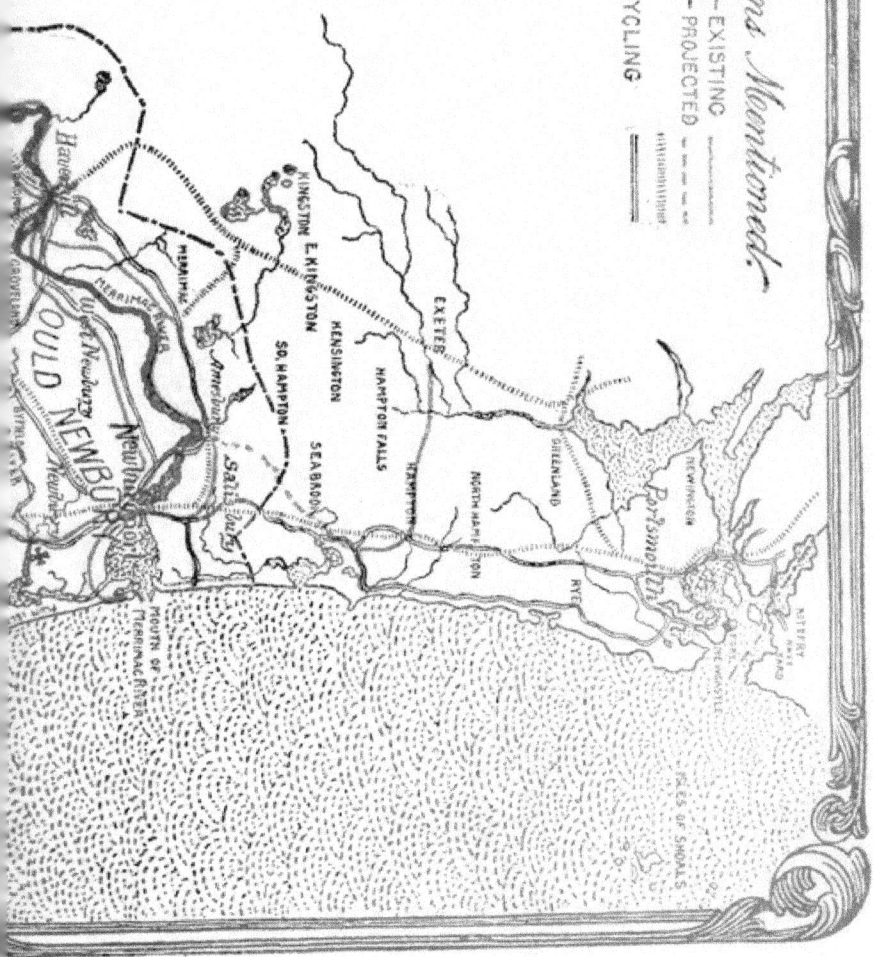

Location of Towns Mentioned.

ELECTRIC ST. RAILWAYS — EXISTING

ELECTRIC ST. RAILWAYS — PROJECTED

STEAM RAILWAYS

HIGHWAYS BEST FOR BICYCLING

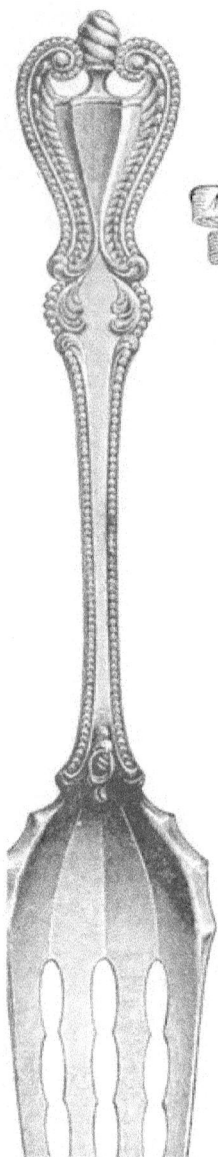

Thebes;" the "Idler," in two volumes; and Volume II of "Letters Written by the late Right Honorable Philip Dorman Stanhope, Earl of Chesterfield," Volume I of which was published at Boston.

The publishers of these were Angier March, successor to Blunt & March, Thomas & Whipple, and John Mycall.

An evidence of the magnitude of this business is the extensive advertising of books in the local papers of that time, and the fact that one of the stores burned in the great fire of 1811, contained a stock of $30,000 worth of books.

Newburyport is, or has been, more or less identified with some of the most prominent educational institutions of the present, first among which is Harvard College. The town of Newbury contributed to the support of this institution in its earliest years, and had the honor of claiming its first graduate, Benjamin Woodbridge of this town being placed at the head of the class of nine who completed the course in 1642.

Position in the class was determined by the standing or rank of the families of members, a method in keeping with the rigid social distinctions of those days.

Newburyport furnished seven professors to Harvard College, including Samuel Webber who was made president in 1806, and Cornelius Conway Felton, who was similarly honored in 1860. Other college presidents born here were Samuel C. Bartlett of Dartmouth, Leonard Woods of Bowdoin, and Benjamin Hale of Hobart.

Dummer Academy, Newbury, was founded by Governor Dummer in 1761, and was the first institution of its kind in operation in America. It has had a notable history, and is still in a flourishing condition.

The Colonial Book

EMINENT MEN OF EARLY TIMES RESIDENT HERE, NOT ELSEWHERE MENTIONED.

Chief Justice Samuel Sewall, the subject of Whittier's poem of which the quotation on the first page of this book is the beginning, was born in 1652, and was one of the most learned and respected men of his time. He married Hannah Hull, daughter of John Hull, master of the Massachusetts Mint, referred to on another page as the first silversmith in Boston, who presented the bride with a dowry equal to her weight, in silver sixpences.

Theophilus Bradbury, a jurist of distinction and member of Congress under Washington's administration, was born here in 1739. He was also justice of the Supreme Court of Massachusetts.

Charles Jackson, a son of Jonathan Jackson, was born in 1775, and became an eminent lawyer and justice of the Supreme Court of Massachusetts.

Patrick Tracy Jackson, born in Newburyport in 1780. Merchant and originator, with his brother-in-law, Francis C. Lowell, of cotton-cloth manufacture in America. They invented machinery, and established a mill at Waltham which was in successful operation many years, and was said to be the first manufactory in the world to combine cotton spinning and weaving, under one roof. Later, Mr. Jackson purchased the entire site and water privilege of the present city of Lowell, which he founded, and named in honor of his brother-in-law and former partner, then dead. In 1830, Mr. Jackson, in company with Mr. Boot, conceived the project of constructing a railroad in New England, and, overcoming great obstacles, completed it in 1835. This was the Boston & Lowell Railroad, now a part of the Boston & Maine system.

Charles Toppan, the first president of the American Bank Note Company, was born in 1796, and studied engraving in Philadelphia. He was later associated with Jacob Perkins, with whom he went to England to introduce improvements in bank-note engraving. In 1858, he organized the American Bank Note Company of New York, with branches in Boston, Philadelphia, Cincinnati, New Orleans, and Montreal.

Jacob Little, son of a prosperous merchant of Newburyport, was born in 1797, and at an early age entered the employ of

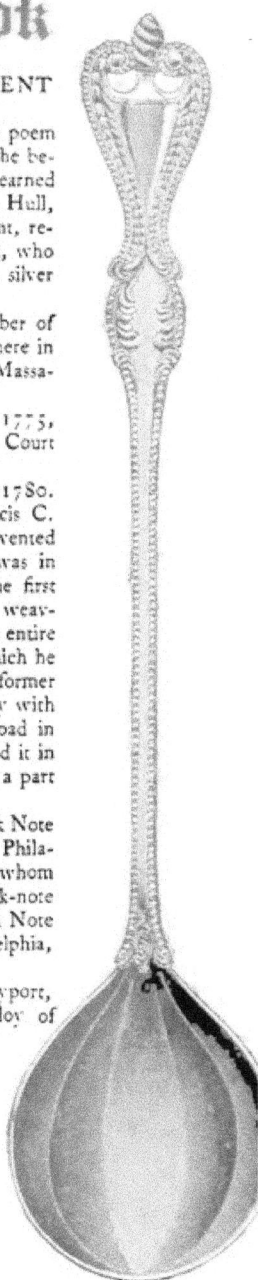

Pickering House
Salem

a prominent merchant of New York. He afterward became a member of the New York Stock Exchange, and was the acknowledged head of the financial world of that city.

William Wheelwright, one of Newburyport's greatest benefactors, was born In 1798. He was a ship-master, and was cast away on the coast of Brazil in 1823; which led him to settle and engage in business in South America, in the development of which he became a prominent factor. He established steamship lines and built the first railroads on that continent, overcoming tremendous natural obstacles, and finally accumulating great wealth. His statue in bronze stands in the public square of Valparaiso, the gift of the people, in recognition of his achievements.

He always retained his attachment for and interest in his native town, and in his will provided for the establishment of a scientific school here, when the fund, which now amounts to $400,000, should be sufficient. A part of the income of this sum is now used to defray the expenses of a scientific education for such graduates of the High School as desire it, some being maintained in Europe for this purpose.

Caleb Cushing, the eminent lawyer and statesman, was born in Salisbury in the year 1800, but came to Newburyport with his parents at the age of two years. He was educated for the bar, and early achieved distinction in his profession. He was minister to China and to Spain, and represented this country at the Geneva tribunal.

He was also commissioned brigadier general in the Mexican War, and held many other important offices.

Others whom Newburyport has been proud to call her sons by birth or adoption are:—

Right Reverend Thomas M. Clarke, Bishop of Rhode Island, born here in 1812.

The Colonial Book

Benjamin Perley Poore, journalist and author, born at Indian Hill Farm, Newbury, the home of his ancestors for many generations, in 1820.

General A. W. Greeley, of the United States Army, commander of the Arctic Expedition bearing his name. He was born in 1844.

Mr. William C. Todd, founder of the Free Reading Room of this city, and lately donor of $50,000 to maintain a free newspaper reading room in the Boston Public Library. Mr. Todd was born in Atkinson, N. H., in 1823; and was for many years principal of the Female High School of this city.

Josiah Little, founder of the Public Library.

Michael Simpson, by whose liberality the Public Library building was greatly enlarged and improved.

George Peabody, the famous London banker, whose benefactions amounted to millions of dollars. Mr. Peabody received his early business training here in the employ of his brother, but was obliged to leave Newburyport after the great fire of 1811. He endowed the Newburyport Public Library with a fund of $15,000.

NOTES.

The quaint old sign of the Wolfe Tavern, pictured at the end of this book, is a pleasing reminder of the ancient institution of that hostelry, as well as a token of early patriotism and tribute to military greatness.

Captain William Davenport brought back from the plains of Abraham enthusiastic appreciation of his late commander, General Wolfe, who fell a sacrifice to bravery in the hour of his hard-earned victory. When, therefore, in 1762, Captain Davenport transformed his dwelling near the lower end of Fish (now State) Street to a tavern, he dedicated it to his lamented leader, and placed in front a swinging sign, elaborately carved, with a portrait of General Wolfe, surrounded by a wreath entwined with scrolls, the whole appropriately painted and gilded. This highly

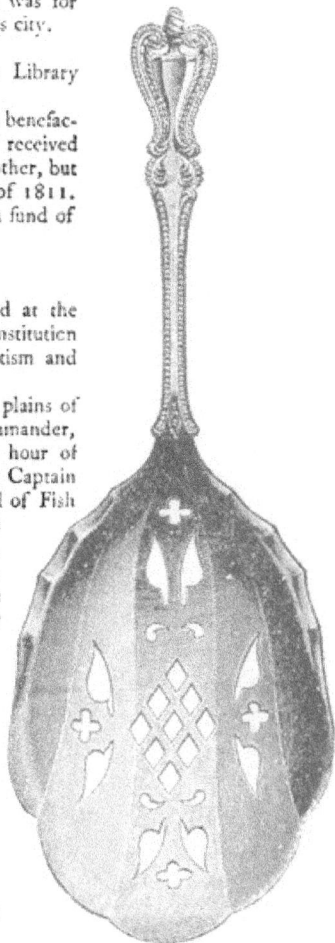

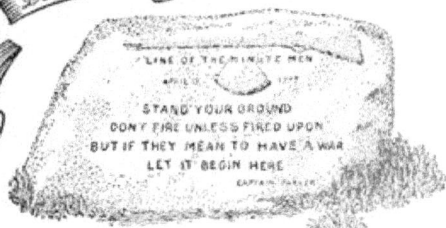

The Colonial Book

decorative emblem was freely threatened with destruction, during the Revolutionary War, when only the hatred of all things British was thought of, and former pride in the achievements of Wolfe forgotten. While all other reminders of royalty were destroyed, and notwithstanding the declaration of a local newspaper, that it was an "insult to the inhabitants of this truly republican town," it remained in place until destroyed by the great fire of 1811. The present sign was erected in 1814, when the tavern was removed to its present location.

Before the introduction of railroads, the Wolfe Tavern was the property, and a station, of the Eastern Stage Company, which ran daily trips, with relays of horses, to Boston and Portsmouth; and the arrival and departure of the stages, which, it may be noted, were all built in Newburyport, were events of considerable importance, and attended with consequent excitement. The Eastern Stage Company was the forerunner of the Eastern Railroad Company, which road is now operated by the Boston & Maine Railroad Company.

The brick building on the corner of State and Harris Streets, which was the nucleus of the present hotel building, was first occupied as a residence by Colonel John Peabody, uncle of George Peabody, and then a merchant in this town.

Two Newburyport men, members of Captain Richard Titcomb's company, were of the number that conveyed Benedict Arnold to the British ship Vulture, in September, 1780, and scorned his offer of promotion, if they would follow him in his then announced desertion from the American to the English forces.

One of the ancient institutions of Newburyport is the office of town-crier. It is now neither appointive nor elective, the present incumbent having, years ago, succeeded to it, and con-

White-Ellery House
Gloucester

Jackson House Portsmouth

tinued without opposition. In early times he commanded attention with a drum, and one of his duties was to escort petty culprits through the principal streets, calling attention to their offences, which they also were sometimes required to proclaim. The business of the present picturesque exemplar is, however, mostly confined to announcements of excursions or entertainments, varied with the promotion of retail trade, and his, "Hear what I have to say!" is preceded by the clang of a large hand-bell. It is doubtful if this functionary survives anywhere else in the United States.

The Curfew Bell, which has recently given its name to a movement to compel the retiring of young people from the streets at nine o'clock in the evening, has, with the exception of a short interval in the last decade, been rung here nightly for one hundred and ninety-two years, and it is indeed a curfew, or signal for retiring, for many people.

The first vessel to display the American flag on the river Thames, was the Count de Grasse, Captain Nicholas Johnson, of this port.

A Newburyport ship, the Indus, was also the first to sail from this country to Calcutta, after the war of 1812, and made the return trip before news of her arrival had otherwise reached here.

A few months later in the same year, another vessel, the Dryad, sailed from here to carry to Calcutta the first five missionaries of the American Board of Foreign Missions, an organization established here by a Newburyport and a Salem clergyman, but which has long since outgrown its early home and removed to broader fields.

The history of ship-building at this port, includes many items of general interest. While it is impossible, through imperfect

registration, to ascertain the exact number of vessels built on the Merrimac, it is probable that, from first to last, the number would be upwards of two thousand.

The water-line model which enabled a designer to more easily and accurately ascertain the lines and sections of his creation, was invented here by a prominent ship-builder, Orlando Merrill, in 1794. The original model of this invention is now preserved in the rooms of the New York Historical Society.

In 1853 the celebrated clipper ship Dreadnaught was built here, a vessel whose remarkable records of crossing the Atlantic in a little more than thirteen days, were nearly equal to those of the first steamships.

Newburyport closed the record of ship-building in Massachusetts, with the launching, in 1882, of the Mary L. Cushing, the last vessel of that class built in this state.

Although the various societies of Daughters of the Revolution are of comparatively recent formation, the spirit which they represent was manifest in Newburyport as early as 1796, as shown from the following from the Impartial Herald of that year.

Newburyport, February 26, 1796. Female patriotism. A number of ladies belonging to this town met on Monday, in honor of the day that gave birth to the man "who unites all hearts," and dedicated a few glasses to the following truly sentimental and highly republican toasts.

1. May our beloved *President* preside at the helm of government longer than we shall have time to tell his years.
2. Mrs. Washington, respected consort of our illustrious chief.
3. May the fair patriots of America never fail to assert their independence, which nature equally dispenses.
4. Maria Charlotte Corday. May each Columbian daughter, like her, be ready to sacrifice their life to liberty.
5. The day that saw the wondrous hero rise shall, more than all our sacred days, be blessed.

House of Seven Gables

Doak House
Doak Lane
Marblehead

WHILE the purpose of this book is to give, in connection with Colonial silverware, an outline of the Colonial and Revolutionary history of Newburyport, it is also designed to note briefly some of the chief points of interest in neighboring cities and towns. This reference to its main object is made that any seeming lack of proportion between the representation of a place and its known importance may be understood, and the random character of the selections accounted for.

Salem is particularly rich in points of interest around which history or tradition has left its charm of romance or pall of tragedy. It was here that occurred the first armed resistance of the Revolution, when, on the 26th of February, 1775, the march of three hundred British troops sent by General Gage to seize munitions of war was arrested. From here came Colonel Timothy Pickering, one of Washington's most trusted advisers, and to whom was given successively every office in his cabinet, when the latter became president.

In addition to its wealth of history and the memories of its once famous commerce, its heroes of war and statecraft, and its merchant princes, Salem is remembered and particularly visited as the home of Hawthorne and the scene of several of his romances. His birthplace, the home of his youth, the "House of Seven Gables," the "Grimshaw House," and Custom House, as well

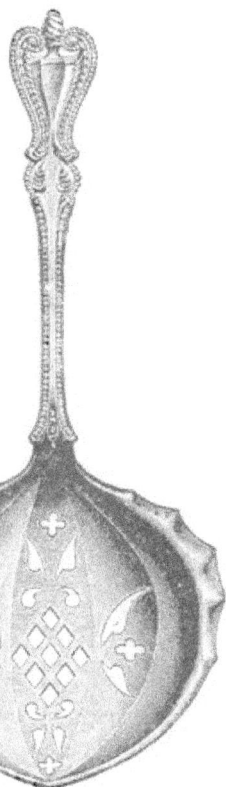

First Church in Salem
1634

as the many other houses and haunts immortalized in his writings, bring to the thoughtful visitor a vivid sense of personal acquaintance, not to be gained alone by the reading of his works. Other cities have historic associations and fine old architecture, have had even the witches — of painful memory — but only Salem can show these originals of storied scenes.

THOUGH small in point of population, Marblehead has strongly marked characteristics, and has played a very important part in the history of our country. Like the other seaport towns of northern Massachusetts, it furnished many men for the navy of the Revolution, and none were braver or hardier than the sons of this rocky and picturesque hamlet. Chief among these was Captain Mugford, to whose memory and that of his crew a memorial has been erected. He captured, off Boston harbor, in May, 1776, a British ship, laden with military supplies; but, after sending this safely to port, was the same day killed, while defending his ship against an attack of the enemy.

Here lived Agnes Surriage, beloved of Sir Henry Frankland, and here also is the scene of Whittier's poem of "Skipper Ireson's Ride," though the story is doubtless largely imaginary.

The old town is said to have been a resort of pirates and buccaneers from the Spanish Main, but it is pleasanter to contemplate its visitors of to-day, the magnificent yachts that rendezvous here from the coast.

Powder House Marblehead

House where First Evening School in America was Instituted. 1810. Beverly.

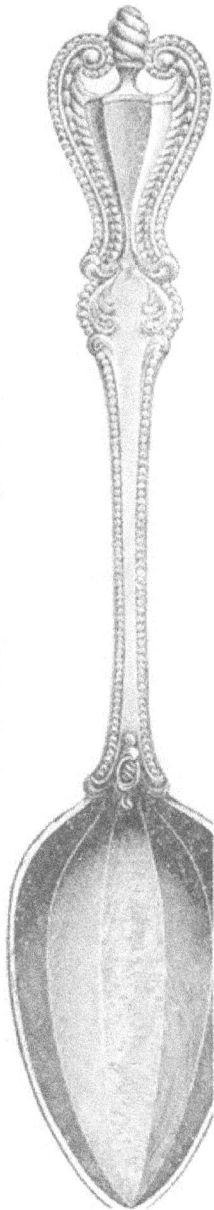

A CROSS the harbor from Marblehead is Beverly, the two arranged like sentinels, guarding the approach to Salem, which is further inland. Marblehead and Beverly divide other honors, for the regiment commanded by Colonel Glover was rec..ited from both places, and took an active part in the Revolution. It was at one time stationed at Beverly, to cover the movements of British men-of-war lying in the outer harbor. This regiment was frequently selected by Washington for enterprises requiring great courage and skill, as instanced by its responsible part in the evacuation of New York by the American army in 1776. Its most notable achievement, however, was the memorable passage of the Delaware, when, on the night of Christmas, 1776, Washington's army was enabled, under the skillful guidance of these men of Marblehead and Beverly, to cross in safety the stormy and ice-filled river, and capture at Trenton a large part of the British army.

Beverly was bombarded by the British ship Nautilus, but suffered no great damage. In return, her privateers, which were early commissioned, brought in many valuable prizes and materially aided the American cause.

A T the time of the Revolution and for the first half of this century, the whole of Cape Ann was known as Gloucester. Since that time the towns of Rockport and Annisquam have been set off, thus reducing the territory of Gloucester.

Fishing, in which it is now supreme, has always been its leading industry, and the "Captains Courageous" of Kipling were no less so when courage meant the braving of hostile guns as well as tempest and rocky shores.

The Colonial Book

A Newburyport privateer, the Yankee Hero, reinforced by Gloucester sailors, was captured, off the Cape, by a British man-of-war, disguised as a merchantman, after a hard fought battle. Among the noted patriots of those days, Captain Harraden of Gloucester was a famous and successful fighter who did great service for his country.

On the southerly side of the entrance to Gloucester harbor, lies the reef of Norman's Woe—remembered in Longfellow's "Wreck of the Hesperus"—the ceaseless peal of the floating bell warning the mariner of its menacing presence, as when, on that fatal night of old, the skipper's daughter cried:—

> "O father! I hear the church-bells ring,
> O say, what may it be?"

ONE of the most interesting of neighboring cities is Portsmouth. From the earliest time it has been fortified, and later its fine deep harbor led to the establishment of the Navy Yard and attendant government institutions.

All the prevalent sentiments of liberty and independence noted in accounts of other places were characteristic of Portsmouth, though the town had probably a greater number of prominent loyalists than any other, save Boston. They were roughly handled by the patriots, and at the outbreak of open hostilities were obliged to seek safety elsewhere.

One of the first decisive acts of the Revolution, if not the first, was successfully consummated here, on the night of December 14, 1774, four months before the battle of Lexington.

On that night, a party of men, anticipating the garrisoning of Fort William and Mary, at Newcastle, by the forces of the king, descended on the fort, surprising and overpowering the sentinel and commandant, forced its surrender, and removed to Portsmouth upwards of one hundred barrels of gunpowder and fifteen of the lightest cannon. The munitions were effectively used in the Revolution, a large part of the gunpowder being sent to Cambridge.

Portsmouth was markedly aristocratic in early times, and the elegant Colonial mansions that still adorn its streets are reminders of the days of affluence, when, like Newburyport and Salem, it gloried in a large foreign trade or hoarded the gains of privateering.

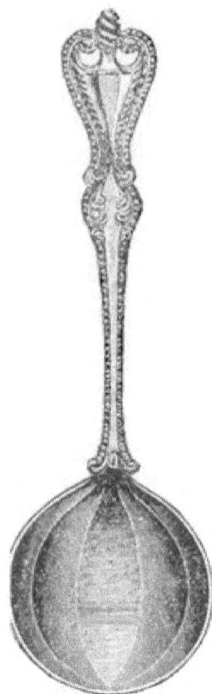

The Colonial Book

HAVERHILL, which is to-day a populous and busy city, lacked the advantages of the coast towns, and although settled in 1640, did not reach its present development until the era of manufacturing had superseded that of commerce. It was, however, notably active in the events leading up to the Revolution, and furnished, both promptly and willingly, its full quota of men and funds for that war.

In earlier times, Haverhill suffered severely from Indian attacks, its inland situation rendering it particularly liable to this danger. The most famous of these took place on the fifteenth of March, 1697, when thirty-nine persons were killed or captured, and a number of houses burned. Among those taken prisoners were, Hannah Duston—whose husband, Thomas Duston, fought his way to safety, with seven of their eight children—and Mary Neff, her nurse. After traveling some days and suffering many hardships, they were brought to an island in the Merrimac, situated a few miles above what is now Concord. Early on the morning of April 30, while the savages all slept, Mrs. Duston aroused her nurse and an English youth who had been longer a prisoner, and, arming themselves with tomahawks, they killed their captors, to the number of ten, a squaw and youth escaping. After scuttling all the canoes but one, they provisioned that and started back to Haverhill, but, before going far, decided to return and scalp the Indians, as evidence of their deed; this they did, finally reaching home in safety. One of the features of Haverhill is the Hannah Duston monument commemorating this event.

A FEW miles from Newburyport, in the town of Amesbury, is the home of Whittier's later years, and from there, in 1892, he was buried, the simple service attended by a gathering of genius such as few occasions could attract.

An interesting reminder of Whittier, in Amesbury, is the "Captain's Well," the subject of his poem of that name. It was constructed by Captain Bagley, in or about 1794.

> "I will dig a well for the passers-by,
> And none shall suffer from thirst, as I."

A S active revolution had its beginning in the battles of Concord and Lexington, battles which filled the roads from far and near with hurrying minute-men, pressing

eagerly to the aid of their heroic compatriots, we have included illustrations of a few of the many historic buildings and commemorative monuments identified with this uprising, with which these towns abound.

All the towns here written of, and many others, share in a degree, with Concord and Lexington, the glory of these monuments; for, while only those favored by proximity arrived in time to take part in the fighting, all responded immediately to the alarm.

SOME PLACES OF HISTORIC INTEREST IN NEWBURYPORT AND VICINITY WHICH MAY BE REACHED BY ELECTRIC CARS.

NEWBURYPORT IS SITUATED AT THE MOUTH OF THE MERRIMAC RIVER, WHICH JOINS THE ATLANTIC ON THE NORTH SHORE OF MASSACHUSETTS BAY, THIRTY-SEVEN MILES FROM BOSTON, AND IS REACHED BY TWO DIVISIONS OF THE BOSTON AND MAINE RAILROAD, FROM THE NORTHERN UNION STATION, CAUSEWAY STREET, BOSTON.

Parker river, named for Rev. Thomas Parker, one of the first settlers who landed on its north shore in 1635. About four miles from railroad station.

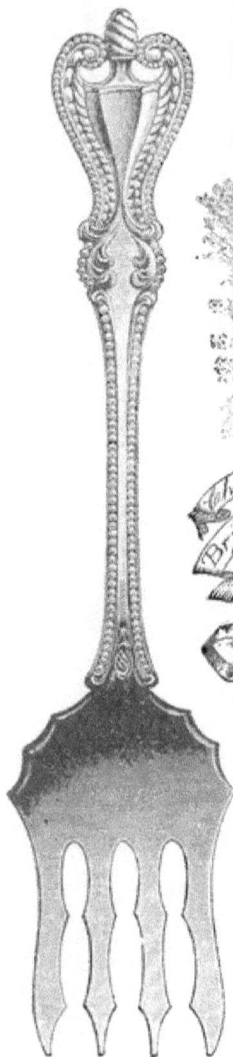

The Colonial Book

The picturesque Spencer-Pierce house, also called the "Garrison House," built by Daniel Pierce about 1670, on a farm of four hundred acres laid out to John Spencer in 1635.

"Trayneing Green," laid out in 1642. Scene of the encampment of Quebec expedition under Benedict Arnold, September, 1775, and location of a boulder and bronze tablet commemorating the event.

The Noyes house on Parker Street, built about the year 1646 by Rev. James Noyes associate pastor with Rev. Thomas Parker. Near by is the old elm of Newbury, a tree of romantic origin, and the subject of a poem by Hannah Flagg Gould.

The Coffin house, High Street, occupied by Tristram Coffin, in 1653, and afterwards the residence of Joshua Coffin, the historian of Newbury, also remembered as Whittier's "Village Schoolmaster." Still occupied by descendants of the original owner.

The Illsley house, High Street, near head of Marlborough Street, built in 1670, and at one time a tavern. Near by, from 1653 to 1755, was the Blue Anchor Tavern, the most important of early inns.

House No. 65 High Street, owned and occupied by Caleb Cushing at the time of his death.

First Presbyterian meeting house, Federal Street, erected in 1756 and rebuilt in 1856. Here Rev. George Whitefield, the great evangelist, preached and was buried, in a vault under the pulpit.

Nos. 3 and 5 School Street, the house where William Lloyd Garrison was born.

Nos. 9 and 11 School Street, the house where Rev. George Whitefield died.

Bomb-shell, on a stone post at the corner of Middle and Independence Streets. Brought from Louisburg by Nathaniel Knapp, after the capture of that fortress, in 1758.

Market Square. On the southeasterly side stood the house owned by William Morse, whose wife, Goody Morse, was, in 1679, convicted of witchcraft and sentenced to death; but, the people becoming more enlightened, the sentence was not executed.

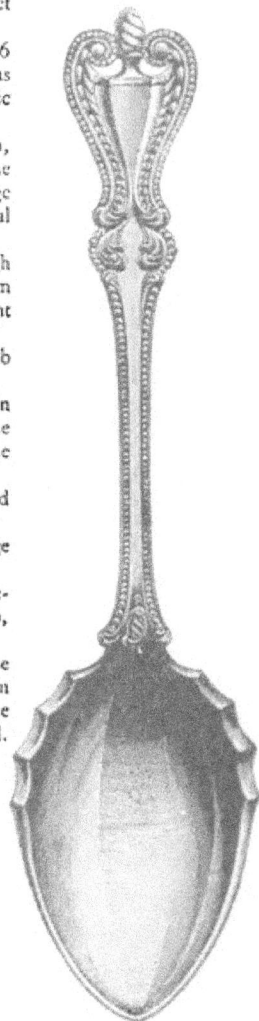

The Colonial Book

This was probably the first case of trial and conviction for witch craft in Massachusetts.

Rooms of Newburyport Marine Society, State Street, organ ized in 1772; containing curiosities gathered by members. Open to visitors from 10 to 12 A. M., 2 to 4 P. M.

No. 21 Charter Street, for many years the residence of Hannah Flagg Gould, author of several volumes of prose and poetry.

Public Library building, erected in 1771 by Patrick Tracy, a prominent merchant, as a residence for his son, Nathaniel Tracy also a merchant and ship owner who attained wide prominence by reason of the magnitude of his operations and the magnificence of his living. Washington occupied apartments in this house in 1789, and Lafayette was entertained here in 1824. In 1865 the building was purchased and adapted for the present use and was added to in 1882, by the generosity of Michael Simpson. On the first floor are: a free reading room, maintained for many years through the liberality of William C. Todd, Esq., and the rooms of the Historical Society of Old Newbury, where visitors may inspect objects of historic interest. Some of the rooms on this floor retain their original character.

Dalton house, No 95 State Street, built in 1750, and occu pied by Tristram Dalton, the first senator to congress from Massachusetts. Was later occupied by Moses Brown, a wealthy merchant. Now owned and occupied by the Dalton Club.

Frog Pond and Bartlett Mall, now included in Washington Park, were first improved in 1800, through the exertions and liberality of Captain Edmund Bartlett.

The Court House stands on this Mall, and nearly opposite is the Putnam Free School building, one of the earliest and most liberal institutions of its kind. At the easterly end of the Park is a statue of Washington by J. Q. A. Ward, presented to the city by Daniel I. Tenney.

House No. 34 Green Street, built in 1879 by Hon. Theo philus Parsons, an eminent jurist, with whom John Quincy Adams and Robert Treat Paine studied law, and occupied by him until 1800.

Brown Square, given to the city by Moses Brown in 1802.
The statue of William Lloyd Garrison was presented to the
city by William H. Swasey, Esq., and is by David M. French
of Newburyport.

Meeting house of the First Religious Society, Pleasant Street,
built in 1800. A fine example of early architecture, with
characteristic interior.

High Street, St. Paul's Church. The first building was
erected here in 1738, and was taken down in the year 1800, to
make room for the present edifice. Right Rev. Edward Bass,
D.D., was at that time rector of the church, and was the first
bishop of the diocese of Massachusetts and Rhode Island. It has
many interesting architectural features, and also a bell made by
Paul Revere.

Dexter house, No. 201 High Street, built by Jonathan Jackson in 1772, and later purchased and occupied by "Lord"
Timothy Dexter, a wealthy and eccentric character, by whom
it was adorned with many wooden statues, since removed. It
was purchased in 1874 by Mr. George H. Corliss, the renowned
engine builder, and occupied by his family until recently.

Lowell-Johnson house, No. 203 High Street, built about 1774
by John Lowell, son of Rev. John Lowell, who was afterwards
judge of the United States Circuit Court. He was the father of
Francis Cabot Lowell, for whom the city of Lowell was named,
grandfather of the founder of the Lowell Institute of Boston, and
also grandfather of James Russell Lowell. The house was later
occupied by John Tracy, son of Patrick Tracy, and he entertained
here, in 1782, the Marquis de Castellux, Baron Talleyrand,
and other officers of the French army.

House No. 244 High Street, frequently the home of John G.
Whittier during the last years of his life.

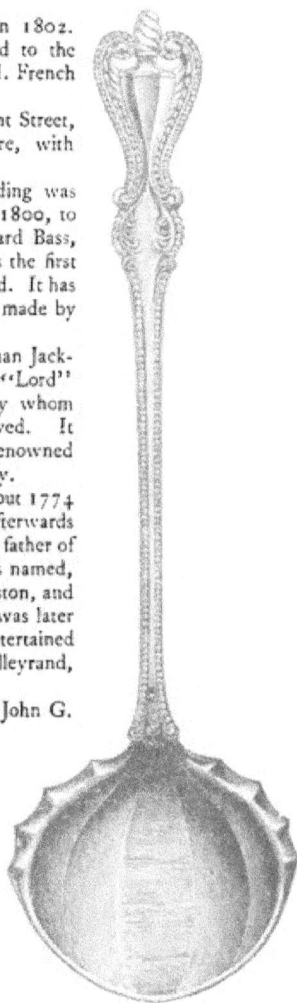

Little River Bridge

The Toppan house, No. 10 Toppan Street, built by Jacob Toppan in 1670, and still in possession of his lineal descendants.

House northeasterly corner of Oakland and High Streets, was owned and occupied by James Parton.

Pillsbury place, No. 265 High Street. This was first the farm of Edward Rawson, clerk of the town and member of the House of Deputies. Later, he was for thirty-five years secretary of the Colony of Massachusetts Bay. In 1651 it was by him sold to Job C. Pillsbury, who in 1700 erected a dwelling house, which was destroyed by fire in 1889, and of which the present structure, owned and occupied by his descendants, is a copy.

Essex, Merrimac, or "Chain" Bridge. Here in 1792 was erected the first bridge across the Merrimac river. It was, in 1810, superseded by the present suspension bridge, which was the second of its kind in the country.

Deer Island, home of Harriet Prescott Spofford. The house here was, in the early part of the century, a noted tavern and toll-house for the bridges on either side.

Garrison House
Haverhill

The Colonial Book

Among the most interesting spots to be found are the old burial grounds with their curious and quaintly inscribed head-stones, memorials in many cases of famous characters, and in themselves a written history of many early events. Those most easily reached are: —

The Burying Ground of the First Parish, High Street, near "Trayneing Green." Many of the first settlers are buried here.

The Old Hill Burying Ground and the New Hill Burying Ground, both on Pond Street, near Washington Park. Here are buried many once prominent in local and national affairs.

St. Paul's Church-yard, High Street.

Burying Ground of the Second Parish, Sawyer's Hill.

Belleville Cemetery, formerly churchyard of Queen Anne's Chapel, the first building of the Episcopal Church.

Oak Hill Cemetery, State Street, consecrated in 1842, is the most important modern burying ground, and is noteworthy for the beauty of its situation and arrangement, as well as for its entrance gates and many fine monuments.

For much of the information contained in the above list the compiler is indebted to a volume entitled, "OULD NEWBURY," by John J. Currier. Published by Damrell and Upham, Boston, Mass.

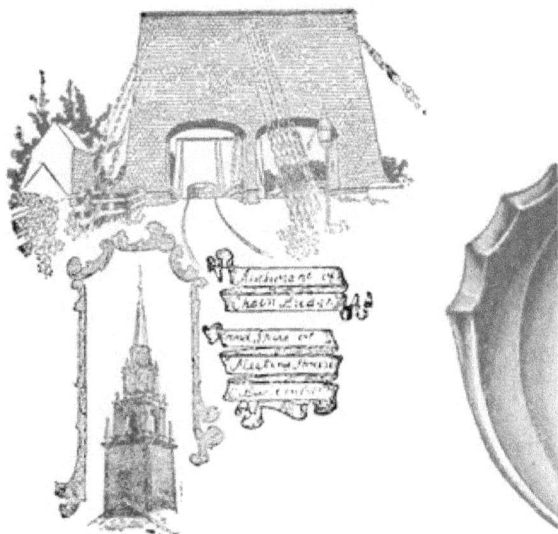

This little book was arranged and printed for the
TOWLE MFG. COMPANY, *Silversmiths*
by WILL BRADLEY, *at the* UNIVERSITY PRESS
Cambridge, U. S. A.

One Hundred and Sixtieth Thousand

THE COLONIAL PATTERN

IS MADE IN STERLING SILVER (925·1000 FINE), AND SOLD ONLY BY LEADING JEWELERS IN THE UNITED STATES AND PROVINCES, FROM WHOM MAY BE OBTAINED A CATALOGUE ILLUSTRATING UPWARDS OF ONE HUNDRED ARTICLES OF TABLE FLAT-WARE. THE CATALOGUE WILL BE MAILED TO ANY ADDRESS UPON REQUEST. ✒ ✒ BUYERS OF SILVERWARE SHOULD CAREFULLY EXAMINE THE TRADE MARK WHICH IS A GUARANTEE OF QUALITY.

TRADE MARK

STERLING

TOWLE MFG. COMPANY
NEWBURYPORT & CHICAGO

James Wolfe Esg.
1762.

www.ingramcontent.com/pod-product-compliance
Lightning Source LLC
Chambersburg PA
CBHW032140080426
42733CB00008B/1137